HOW TO BECOME A BETTER NEGOTIATOR

The WorkSmart Series

HOW TO BECOME A BETTER NEGOTIATOR

James G. Patterson

AMERICAN MANAGEMENT ASSOCIATION
THE WORKSMART SERIES

New York • Atlanta • Boston • Chicago • Kansas City • San Francisco • Washington, D.C.
Brussels • Toronto • Mexico City

Library of Congress Cataloging-in-Publication Data

Patterson, James G.
    How to become a better negotiator / James G. Patterson.
        p.   cm.—(WorkSmart series)
    Includes bibliographical references.
    ISBN 0-8144-7839-5
    1. Negotiation in business.   I. Title.   II. Series.
HD58.6.P38   1996
658.4—dc20   95-51787
                                              CIP

Printing number

10   9   8   7   6   5   4

CONTENTS

PREFACE

If you think about it, you'll realize that you negotiate all the time, every day. You negotiated to get your job and a raise. You negotiate with coworkers about where to have lunch. You negotiate with your spouse and other loved ones about where to take a vacation. Almost all of us have negotiated the purchase of an automobile or a house.

Most of us *hate* to negotiate. Why is that? For one thing, negotiation isn't a skill we were taught, like writing or reading. We were supposed to just "pick it up." Our discomfort may also result from unpleasant experiences with negotiation. Or it may stem from our upbringing; weren't we all taught to try to get along, to avoid confrontation, to want to be liked? Some of us may see negotiation as a war and worry about ruining a relationship without even getting what we want.

The goal of winning negotiations ought to be a "win-win" outcome in which both sides feel they got the best deal possible. Win-win deals preserve and even enhance ongoing long-term relationships.

The old way of thinking was to see negotiating as a win-lose or a lose-lose battle of wills. Win-win negotiating, in contrast, is based on honesty and effective communication so that both sides can get what they want most, or at least more than they expect to get.

Take the tale of two sisters squabbling over an orange. They can't agree on a way to divide the orange, so their mother cuts it in half and gives one piece to each sister. The first sister takes her half, eats the fruit, and throws away the peel; the second sister throws away the fruit and uses the peel for a cake. Both sisters failed to understand the other's interests and focused instead on their own positions. Had they been willing to communicate, one could have had a whole fruit and the other a whole peel. Instead, they both got less than they wanted.

Negotiating effectively really is nothing more than common sense and communication. You *can* learn to be a good negotiator if:

- You know what you want and what you are willing to give up.
- You know (or have a good idea) what the other side wants and what it is willing to give up.
- You come to the table with a *how can we both win* attitude.
- You are skilled in the negotiating essentials of problem solving, listening, and basic conflict management and in the uses of tactics and strategies in negotiating.

This book contains five chapters, each building upon those preceding:

- Chapter 1, "Communication Styles and Negotiating." This chapter will show you what primary communication style you use, what characteristics (both good and bad) are associated with that style, how to accentuate the positives and minimize the negatives of your style, and how to judge your opponents' styles.

- Chapter 2, "Listening as a Primary Negotiating Tool." Most of us assume that we know how to listen. After all, we have two ears, don't we? You will learn that listening is not the same as hearing, and that it takes a lot more to listen effectively than simply to hear. You'll learn whether or not you are a good listener and how you can be a better listener to maximize your negotiating results.

- Chapter 3, "Understanding Conflict Management." Here you'll learn why so many of us hate conflict and negotiating. You'll learn your preferred style of handling conflict situations, how to use each of the five conflict resolution styles effectively, and how to use a five-step problem-solving method to handle conflict and negotiations.

• Chapter 4, "Being More Assertive in Negotiating." You will discover how assertive you are, learn that assertiveness is *not* the same as aggressiveness, and find out how to use various strategies to handle difficult people and situations.

• Chapter 5, "Getting Down to Business: Let's Negotiate!" By this point, you've built up the skills necessary to learn the basics of win-win negotiating. In this chapter you'll learn what goes into planning negotiations. You will find out the importance of time, power, information, and context. You'll learn the common mistakes made by neophyte negotiators and how to avoid them. You'll also discover how to use various tactics and how to counteract the tactics of others when you negotiate. Finally, you'll learn about negotiating long-lasting win-win deals internationally.

HOW TO
BECOME A
BETTER
NEGOTIATOR

CHAPTER 1

COMMUNICATION STYLES AND NEGOTIATING

To negotiate effectively, you need to be on the same wavelength as your opponent. You also need to know what negotiating style you naturally prefer. But what often happens is that we don't care about people's styles, and that causes unhealthy conflict. You may think the other person is a jerk. But before you rush to judgment, consider that the problem may be that you're trying to communicate with a style different from the one that the other person is comfortable using. Kind of like what the character actor Struther Martin uttered in the movie *Cool Hand Luke:* "What we have here is a failure to communicate!"

Differences in communication style can explain why a carefully crafted presentation works for one team or person and doesn't for another. A good negotiator understands that all people don't have the same kind of brain. The best negotiators strive to use a variety of styles to accomplish the same thing; instead of trying to negotiate with all people the same way, they try to reach people the way they're used to being reached.

The four communication styles: Creator, Thinker, Listener, and Doer

There is a body of research that supports the existence of individual differences in styles of learning and communicating. In the 1920s the Swiss psychoanalyst Carl Jung asserted that people develop and use one dominant behavior style. Although, over the course of time, people tend to use a blend of styles, one style predominates. Other researchers, like the American psychologist Paul Mot, have suggested that people behave, communicate, and learn according to one of four styles: creator, thinker, listener, and doer.

1

We all are a mixture of communication styles. Nobody is a pure creator, thinker, listener, or doer. There are no right or good styles. Styles are just styles. No one is trapped by a dominant style. However, we all need to recognize our dominant style, understand the negatives associated with that style (the negatives come out when we are tired or stressed), work on fighting those negatives, understand the dominant styles of the people we deal with, and learn to "flex" to those other styles. This is called getting on the same wavelength.

COMMUNICATION STYLE QUIZ

To learn what dominant communication style you use, take the following unscientific test. Read each phrase and check the one word that best describes you. Then count up the check marks in each of the four columns. At the end of the quiz, you'll find the scoring key.

1.	Your manner is basically	*accepting*	*friendly*	*controlling*	*evaluative*
2.	Decision making	*slow*	*emotional*	*impulsive*	*fact-based*
3.	Talk about	*personal things*	*people*	*achievements*	*organization*
4.	Using time	*not rushed*	*socializer*	*rushed*	*runs late*
5.	Relates to others	*accepting*	*empathizer*	*commands*	*assessing*
6.	Gestures	*sparse*	*open*	*impatient*	*closed*
7.	Clothing preferences	*conforms*	*very stylish*	*formal*	*conservative*
8.	Work pace	*steady*	*enthusiastic*	*fast*	*controlled*
9.	Listening	*interested*	*distracted*	*impatient*	*selective*
10.	Work area has	*keepsakes*	*pictures*	*awards*	*charts*
11.	Oriented toward	*support*	*people*	*results*	*facts*
12.	Basic personality	*easygoing*	*outgoing*	*dominating*	*no-nonsense*
13.	Communication	*low-key*	*animated*	*direct*	*reserved*
14.	Responsive to others	*steady*	*friendly*	*restless*	*distant*

TOTALS =   **I = _____**   **II = _____**   **III = _____**   **IV = _____**
                      (Listener)   **(Creator)**   **(Doer)**   **(Thinker)**

Scoring Key
7 or more = Strong preference   5–6 = Moderate preference   0–2 = Low preference

Now you should have a good idea of what dominant style you use. What if you don't have a dominant style (seven or more checks in one area)? Having three or four checks in all four styles may indicate that you have an easier time than most of us communicating with all kinds of people. Those with a couple of moderate scores and one or two very low scores probably have the hardest time communicating with people who are strongest in their low-scoring (0 to 2) areas.

COMMUNICATION STYLE CHARACTERISTICS

What are the characteristic of these communication styles? What are the best ways to communicate with people with each of these styles? As you read about the characteristics of each style, enter in the matrix in Figure 1 the name or names of people you negotiate with or otherwise have to deal with who you think fit that style:

Style I: The Listener

These folks are people–oriented. Listeners believe that there is more than one method for producing the same results. They demand a voice in decisions that affect them. Listeners can be slow decision makers. They want to talk about the issues and get to know you as a person. They also don't

Figure 1. The four communication styles.

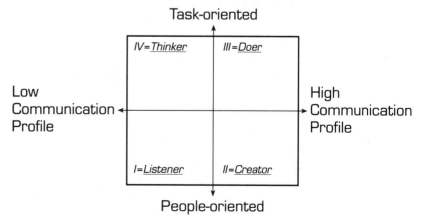

delegate very well (perhaps afraid of "offending" somebody by asking?). They are people persons. They place a high premium on relationships. Because of this, they often make the best mediators and team builders. But they just can't say no. Everybody's priorities are their priorities. Perhaps because of this, they can get easily sidetracked. They seek security in their job and are not big risk takers. And, they would be the last people (along with thinkers) to volunteer to make a presentation!

Listeners can improve their relationships with others by being more assertive, forcing themselves to focus less on relationships and more on tasks, and learning to make observations based on fact, not subjective judgments.

In negotiations, listeners turn into pacifiers, always seeking to make all sides happier.

You can negotiate more successfully with listeners if you can clearly identify their objective. The listeners will then reach the objective in their own way. When given the freedom to do so, these people like to prove themselves. Try to be more casual and personal with them. Be relaxed, and show interest in them as people. Know that when listeners are stressed, they are often submissive and indecisive. Slow down and reassure them.

Listeners have the most conflict with doers.

Style II: The Creator

Creators are enthusiastic and excitement-driven people. And that excitement is often catching. They don't mind breaking away from the negotiations and having fun. They also like to be admired and love to speak in public (whether or not they know what they're talking about). But sometimes they just won't shut up. Creators can be impulsive and often make decisions on the spot. They're very persuasive and optimistic folks. They are idea people and are very creative, but sometimes they resemble the Michael Keaton character in the movie *Night Shift*. Keaton played a character called "The Blaze" who was a self-styled "idea man." He constantly barraged the co-star of the movie, Henry Winkler, with idea after idea for businesses and inventions, finally driving Winkler's character to say to Keaton's character, "You have all these great ideas, but you never follow through on any of them." That is one of the negatives associated with creators—they have a problem with follow-through. The thrill for them is the idea; later they tend to lose interest. In addition, they tend to be priority jumpers. When stressed, creators often try to change the subject. Finally, creators often bring an unusual, yet often welcome, sense of humor to any organization.

Creators can communicate better with others by slowing down and being a little less enthusiastic and intense.

You can communicate better with creators by understanding their need to be recognized. They dislike routine and enjoy fast-paced conversations. Get them excited about a project first; they will then enthusiastically sell others. Then be ready for a fast decision reflecting their excitement.

Creators tend to have the most conflict with thinkers.

Style III: The Doer

Doers are pragmatic, assertive, results-oriented, competitive, and competent. They are no-nonsense, take-charge, get-it-done'rs. Like creators, they are very verbal. Some would say the eagle just loves an audience. Doers tend to be excellent problem solvers, and they take the biggest risks (which can be a negative if they take wild risks or a positive if they learn to take calculated risks). On the negative side, they may be arrogant and domineering, lack trust in others, exhibit short-range thinking, and act without thinking. They can be abrupt and dictatorial, and they can be bad listeners. They tend to be time-conscious people who want information and nothing else. Do you see that person constantly glancing at a clock? Best bet is he or she is a doer.

When doers negotiate, they tend to be "street fighters." They can find it hard to play "win-win" negotiating (discussed in Chapter 5) because they can be unconcerned with others' needs. They negotiate so that they'll win, often at others' cost.

Doers can communicate better with others by listening. Somebody once said, "Perhaps God invented us with two ears and one mouth to use in proportion." Knowing that being stressed or tired tends to make them abrupt, they have to learn to slow down and count to ten before responding. Doers should also strive to allow others to participate at negotiating sessions. Doers normally have to work at showing their feelings, being interested in relationships, and being more open.

How can you get along better with doers? They want their information "bottom line up front." Get to the point quickly with these folks; don't waste their time. Be results-oriented, and don't bog them down with a lot of details. Expect a fast decision based on facts and logic.

Doers tend to have the greatest conflict with listeners.

Style IV: The Thinker

Thinkers think they are very wise. They are the detail people, much like the Mr. Spock character of *Star Trek* fame. They can be slow deciders ("let's run the numbers one more time") because they are always looking for the perfect answer. In fact, others would say of the thinker, "What we have around here is paralysis by analysis." Thinkers are at home with rules, regulations, and predictability. Unlike doers, thinkers tend to be the lowest risk takers. Thinkers might be described as deliberative, proper, conservative, objective and analytical and as weigher of alternatives. They can also be called verbose, indecisive, overly serious, and rigid.

Thinkers can improve their communication with others by moving faster, showing less need for endless detail, being less rigid about following policies, taking more risks, challenging and facing conflict (and not avoiding it), and showing more personal concern for others.

How can you negotiate better with these folks? Show that you have thought out whatever it is you're trying to tell them. Follow a step-by-step approach in trying to persuade them to your point of view. Use charts and graphs to help thinkers see your method of reasoning. Allow time for them to verify your facts and reasoning. Remember, thinkers are motivated by accuracy, logic, and data.

Thinkers tend to have the most conflict with creators.

PUTTING IT TOGETHER

People naturally prefer to deal with others who share their own negotiating style. Problems arise when negotiators have different styles.

Negotiations between listeners and doers or between creators and thinkers are the hardest.

Negotiations between listeners and doers or between creators and thinkers are the hardest. Doers want listeners to take the facts and make a decision. Listeners want doers to go beyond the facts and care about people. Thinkers believe creators are too flippant and easygoing. Creators feel that thinkers get too bogged down in details.

Now let's suppose that you're trying to connect with a group or an individual. You know that you can increase your chance of reaching people by tailoring your message to their particular primary style. Thus, for the primary "creator" you might say, "How do you react to the basic concepts presented here?" You can rephrase that question for a "thinker" by saying, "Based on your own analysis, how are the facts I've presented relevant?" For "listeners" you might say, "How do you feel about what we've discussed?" And for the "doer," you could say, "I hope I haven't bored you; what's your reaction to my main point?"

Knowing that we don't all learn and communicate in the same way can be of great value to you. With a little practice, you'll understand people's different styles and learn to use a variety of methods to get on your listener's wavelength. This is especially important when your opponents' team shows more than one strong style.

Keep in mind that your favorite negotiating style may not be the best way to reach everybody all the time. Using methods that conflict with your style doesn't come automatically. It will take a while until you get comfortable using another style, but it is worth the effort. There are dangers in thinking that you can neatly fit every person into a rigid style cubbyhole. Remember, although people tend to use one primary style, they can, for short periods of time, use different styles. Consciously try to reach others "where they are," not "where you are." If you do, you'll experience far fewer destructive conflicts and unnecessary stress and elicit a lot more cooperation from everybody you deal with.

THREE NEGOTIATING GAMES

There are three kinds of games that people play while negotiating: *win-lose, lose-lose,* and *win-win.* The style that most often gives you the best deal is, not surprisingly, win-win.

• *Win-Lose.* As the name implies, in this scenario one side wins and the other side loses. The outcome depends on which side has the greater power. People who start out with unwavering positions are setting themselves up for a win-lose outcome. Interestingly enough, the democratic concept of majority rule is based on a win-lose game. If one hundred voters participate in an election and fifty-one people vote yes and win, forty-nine people vote no and lose. This hardly seems the way to build lasting harmony!

• *Lose-Lose.* In this game both sides lose something in the negotiations. The best example of a lose-lose game is compromise. We've always been taught that compromise is a good thing. But think about it. Many times a series of compromises leaves both sides with far less than they needed in the first place. Other examples of the lose-lose game are a union that makes unreasonable demands and winds up forcing a company to close, or two feuding coworkers who both end up losing in the long run, branded "troublemakers" or "poor team players." Try getting a better job with that kind of reference!

- *Win-Win.* This is the best outcome, because it ends in a solution satisfactory to all parties. An effective negotiator should look past conflicting means (*me* vs. *them*) and focus on satisfying ends (*us* vs. *the problem*). When both parties in a negotiation have similar goals, a win-win game is more likely to occur. Achieving this requires a positive open attitude on both sides: yes, we can both get something out of this; the enemy is the problem, not each other; we're flexible enough to know there are several solutions for every problem; we understand each other's positions.

Win-win outcomes aren't always possible. When you can't use a win-win problem-solving method, you'll have to resort to compromise. The situation isn't hopeless, though, especially if you're going to have continuing business dealings with the other side. An honest attempt to learn what the other side wants and to try to satisfy those wants will set the stage for continued goodwill and for knowledge of the other side's needs the next time you meet to negotiate.

CHAPTER REVIEW

Take the following open-book review quiz to find out what you have learned so far.

1. What are the four styles of negotiating?

2. What is your dominant style?

3. What three negative communication characteristics do you need to work on?

_____

_____

_____

4. What is the communication style of the most difficult person you know?

_____

5. What can you do to improve communication with this person?

_____

_____

_____

_____

CHAPTER 2

LISTENING AS A PRIMARY NEGOTIATING SKILL

Do you remember where you were on January 28, 1986? On that day, a worldwide television audience watched in horror as the Challenger space shuttle blew up shortly after takeoff. A government investigation into the explosion and the deaths of the eight crew members found that pressure to go ahead with the launch had interfered with the willingness and the ability of launch officials to listen to the concerns of engineers about the safety of the spacecraft. A presidential investigative team later recommended that the National Aeronautics and Space Administration (NASA) develop plans and policies to improve communication (and listening *is* communication) at all levels of the organization.

WHAT IS LISTENING?

A good listener hears, interprets, evaluates, and reacts.

The Challenger tragedy highlights one of the biggest problems present in any large or small organization—few people practice effective listening techniques. Most of us assume we know what listening is. You heard your boss's order, right? Well, hearing is only the first part of listening. When you physically pick up sound waves with your ears, you are hearing. But listening also involves interpreting what you hear. Then you must evaluate what you have heard, weighing the information and deciding how you'll use it. Finally, on the basis of what you have heard and how you have evaluated the information, you react. So a good listener hears, interprets, evaluates, and reacts.

11

Because of our misconceptions about what listening really is, we end up doing a pretty poor job of it. Studies show that we spend up to 80 percent of our waking hours communicating, and at least 45 percent of that time is spent listening. Other studies have shown that immediately after a ten-minute oral presentation, the average listener understands, evaluates, and properly retains only about half of what was said; within forty-eight hours most people retain only 25 percent of the information they heard.

One reason so many people are bad listeners is that they lack training. Consider the four major communication skills we use everyday: listening, speaking, reading, and writing. Remember, more than one third of our time awake is spent listening, yet listening is the least taught communication skill.

Communication Skill	Proportion of All Communication Skills Used	Teaching Emphasis Ranking
Reading	19%	1
Writing	22%	2
Speaking	26%	3
Listening	33%	4

Why should we care to become better listeners? Because, as the Challenger disaster shows, a failure to listen can cost lives. Listening mistakes can also cost money. If every one of the 100 million-plus workers in the United States were to make a simple $10 listening mistake today, it would cost the country more than over $1 billion! Let's make a conservative estimate that most of those 100 million American workers make an average of two listening mistakes a week at a cost of more than $2 billion. If this is true, taken over a year, simple listening mistakes cost us more than $100 billion!

Better listening can mean less paperwork. Most of us learn not to rely on giving information orally because of all the mistakes that result. The result is that we "memo" everything. Just look at your desk. Couldn't some of that paper-work be eliminated by simply talking to another person? Yes, it could, if only you could be sure that the other person knew how to listen. All of this unnecessary paperwork means that we need more word processors, use more secre-taries' time, and require more file cabinets to store all the notes we write down and get from others. We're not going to magically eliminate the paperwork problem in organiza-tions overnight. But we can improve the situation if we all work to become better listeners.

Leaders should be interested in better listening because it will improve the flow of upward communication. There are a lot of ways we can send messages to the people who work for us but not as many ways for them to communicate up-ward. Supervisors who don't know how to listen may find that few of their staff members will talk freely to them. This hurts morale and keeps supervisors from receiving all the critical information they need to make effective decisions. Even if the upward flow of communications starts, one bad listener along the way can stop or distort the message.

For negotiators, better listening improves decision making and problem solving in conferences and meetings. This is easy to understand if you think of the reasons we hold meet-ings. We meet to exchange views, knowledge, and expertise in order to solve problems. Good listening helps people un-derstand other viewpoints. It also helps keep the group cen-tered on the issue at hand and keeps them from wandering off on irrelevant problems or concerns.

Before suggesting ways on how we can become better lis-teners, let's take a short test. Here are the rules. Read the following story once, and only once. (Don't cheat!) This test works best if you read the following to a friend and have him or her take the test!

You're the manager of a shipping department. One morning the mail brings orders for twenty-five items. The phone rings and a store orders ten more items. The buyer from a depart-ment store phones and says his store is overstocked, so please cancel his order for twenty items. The boss drops by and says fifteen more items should be shipped to another customer. A salesperson comes in and orders twenty items.

Without looking back at the story, answer the following question: *What is the name of the shipping manager?*

How did you do? If you answered correctly, it's because you follow Rule 1 in developing good listening habits: You resisted distractions. The distractions in this story were all the statistics! Other listening situations may call for you to look past a speaker's bad habits and concentrate on her ideas.

By the way, the correct answer to the test is . . . *your name.*

LISTENING RULES

The Sperry Corporation, famous for its concern with listening (the corporate slogan is "We understand how important it is to listen") suggests ten ways to improve your listening ability.

1. Resist distractions.
2. Find areas of interest by asking "What's in it for me?"
3. Judge content, not delivery.
4. Don't be quick to argue or judge until you comprehend.
5. Listen for ideas and central themes, not just facts.
6. Be flexible in your note taking. Use different systems depending on the speaker or subject.
7. Work at listening. Show that you are interested.
8. Exercise your mind by occasionally reading difficult materials. Don't pretend that you are challenging your mind if you read only light recreational materials.
9. Keep your mind open. Don't be too quick to react emotionally to trigger words.
10. Understand that you can think faster than you can speak. You must fight the temptation to daydream with slow or boring speakers. The good listener mentally summarizes, weighs the evidence, and lis-

tens between the lines to the tone of the speaker's voice.

Here are two additional rules to add two more rules to Sperry's ten rules of good listening:

11. If you're interested in having members of your staff become better listeners (and I know you are), ask for it. Let people know how important listening is. Ask for training to help you and your team develop good listening skills.

12. If you ask for good listening, reward it. Make it a part of the evaluation process. Otherwise, nobody will take the importance of listening seriously. Here's a suggestion: After a negotiating session, hold a listening critique. Ask each person to evaluate the listening attention he or she received while speaking. Each person should then evaluate his or her own listening performance.

REFLECTIVE LISTENING

There is one easy-to-learn-and-apply listening method that will make you a better listener and a better negotiator. It is called *reflective listening*. This form of listening is different from the way most of us are used to listening, so it may take some practice before you get good at it.

Reflective listening says to the person you're listening to, "I understand what you're saying and how you must feel." It also allows you to check what you believe you heard against what was said. This can both build rapport and prevent unnecessary conflict.

For instance, a coworker angrily tells you she is having a serious problem with the boss. You reply, "This problem really seems to upset you, doesn't it?" Your comment assures your friend that you're listening and you care.

Here's an exercise you can do with a team member that will teach both of you how to listen reflectively. Take about five minutes to tell your friend about a problem at work. Your friend should, on occasion, paraphrase back to you what he or she has heard and show interest through a nod, a smile, or a comment such as "I see" or "Tell me more." Paraphrasing is nothing more than occasionally repeating in your own words what the other person has said to you.

Using this method has two positive effects during negotiations: It lets you check to make sure your partner has understood what you've been saying, and it reassures you that the other person cares about what you've been saying.

Your team member, the listener, should avoid trying to solve your problem for you. As a listener, he must fight the urge to solve your problem directly and allow you to discover the answer on your own which will make you much more committed to the solution! Directly solving another person's problem is *not* reflective listening!

When you and your team member are done with this exercise, discuss how the technique made you, the speaker, feel. Then ask your friend, the reflective listener, how difficult he found it to paraphrase. You and your friend will discover that being a good reflective listener requires taking an active part in what some consider a passive activity—listening!

When you are finished with this exercise, reverse roles so that you become the reflective listener and your friend becomes the speaker. Then repeat the discussion following the exercise.

Remember, this is a new way of doing business. Expect reflective listening to be difficult the first or second time you do it. But keep in mind the benefits that come from the process.

THREE LISTENING QUIZZES

To find out how a good a listener you are, answer the following three quizzes:

QUIZ ONE

A. Circle the term that best describes you as a listener:

*Superior   Excellent   Above Average   Average
Below Average   Poor   Terrible*

(Most people would say average or less; only a tiny minority would say superior or excellent)

B. On a scale of 0 to 100 (100 = highest), how would you rate yourself as a listener?

_____

(55 would be average)

QUIZ TWO

On a scale of 0 to 100, how would the following people rate you as a listener?

Your best friend? (This would be rated highest. Why??)

Your boss? (Most people think bosses would rate them higher than they would rate themselves!)

A business colleague? (The average is around 55)

Your subordinates? (Again, around 55)

Your spouse? (Newlyweds rate this category highest; old marrieds rate this lowest!)

QUIZ THREE

As a listener, how often do you find yourself engaging in these bad listening habits? Check the appropriate columns. Then tabulate your score using the key below.

Listening Habit	Almost Always	Usually	Some-times	Seldom	Almost Never	*SCORE*
1. Calling the subject uninteresting						
2. Criticizing the speaker's delivery or mannerisms						

Listening Habit	Almost Always	Usually	Some- times	Seldom	Almost Never	*SCORE*
3. Getting overstimulated by something the speaker says						
4. Listening primarily for facts						
5. Trying to outline everything						
6. Faking attention to the speaker						
7. Allowing interfering distractions						
8. Avoiding difficult material						
9. Letting emotion-laden words arouse personal antagonism						
10. Wasting the advantage of thought speed (daydreaming)						

Scoring Key:
Almost always = 2
Usually = 4
Sometimes = 6
Seldom = 8
Almost never = 10
TOTAL SCORE =

The average is 62. It seems that when we break listening down into specific areas, we rate ourselves higher than when we look at listening in general.

How can you use these quizzes to improve your listening? You need to work on any area where you scored 8 or lower. What four top areas do you need to work on the most? Seek out help from a coworker who will give you honest feedback.

1. _____

2. _____

3. _____

4. _____

THE COST OF NOT LISTENING

Finally, here's a story that shows the importance of good listening—and how a listening breakdown can cost:

A down-and-out drifter, hungry for something to eat and willing to work for his meal, walked up to a fancy house. He rang the doorbell and asked the lady of the house for a meal in return for any household chore he could do. "Well, certainly! There is a job you could do for me," the lady said. "Take those two cans of green paint around back and paint my porch." "Be glad to, ma'am," said the drifter. Two hours later, the man returned to the front of the house and said, "Ma'am, I've finished the job, and I'm ready to eat! Oh, by the way, that car I painted was no Porsche; it was a Ferrari!"

By now you should know the importance of and the payoff for having good listening skills. To improve your listening, you have to have a positive attitude and a willingness to work at it. Good listening is not just a matter of hearing.

CHAPTER REVIEW

To discover what you have learned so far, take the following open book review quiz.

1. What is listening?

   _____

2. Name three benefits of better listening for negotiators:

   _____

   _____

   _____

3. What are Sperry's ten rules of listening?

    _____

    _____

    _____

    _____

    _____

4. What is reflective listening? What are the benefits of reflective listening?

    _____

    _____

    _____

CHAPTER 3

UNDERSTANDING CONFLICT MANAGEMENT

Anytime you bring two or more people together to solve a problem or make a decision—that is, to negotiate—you may well end up with conflict. Conflict is inevitable. Even the best meaning people will engage in conflict.

Is conflict bad? Not necessarily. But unmanaged conflict can be harmful to us as individuals and to our organization.

Conflict, if handled right, can be a good thing.

Conflict, if handled right, can be a good thing. The Chinese language represents this point well. The Chinese symbol for crisis is made up of two characters: danger and opportunity. A poorly handled conflict can be dangerous; relationships may suffer and productivity may decline. But a skillfully handled conflict can be beneficial. It can function as a safety valve, letting people vent frustrations, and it can lead to solutions for troublesome problems. As the author James Baldwin once said, "Nothing can be changed until it is faced." Rarely will avoiding conflict lead to its resolution; most conflicts won't just go away. But effective conflict management can lead to increased cohesion and loyalty. Facing problems together often brings people closer together, as when two parties spend time and energy trying to negotiate a deal. Consider, for example, the bond that develops between soldiers who have gone through war together.

Why do we have conflicts? There are several good reasons. One is the interdependence that exists between people, departments, and organizations. Conflicts also arise because negotiators bring different objectives to the table. Other reasons for conflict include competition for resources, personal difficulties, and game playing.

Unmanaged conflict carries a high cost. If left unmanaged, stress can lead to health problems, divert energy, time, and resources from legitimate and important personal and organizational goals, and result in corporate sabotage and financial and emotional problems.

To learn how to manage conflict effectively, it's a good idea to learn more about how you personally handle conflict.

QUIZ: HOW DO YOU NATURALLY HANDLE CONFLICT?

Directions: Read the following statements and circle only the numbers next to the questions that describe how you handle conflict. For instance, if you agree with the first statement in the survey, circle both numbers to the right of the question (1 and 1). When you're finished, add up all the circled numbers under "concern for people" and divide that number by the number of questions you agreed with. Then add up all the circled numbers under "concern for production" and divide by the number of questions you agreed with. You will then have an average score for "concern for people" and an average score for "concern for production." Then plot your average conflict scores on the table at the end of the survey.

	Concern for People	Concern for Production
1. Maintains neutrality at all costs; views conflict as a worthless and punishing experience (w/a)	1	1
2. Feels a high concern for people regardless of the production of results and therefore tries to smooth over or ignore conflicts in an attempt to keep everybody happy (s/a)	9	1

	Concern for People	Concern for Production
3. Views production of results (usually his or her own personal goals) as much more important than people and sees nothing wrong with using force when necessary (f/c)	1	9
4. Believes that everyone should have an equal chance to express opinions (c)	5	5
5. Gives equal consideration to people and production of results (ps/c)	9	9
6. Removes self either physically or mentally from groups experiencing any type of conflict; stays away from any situation that might possibly produce conflict (w/a)	1	1
7. Believes that surface harmony is important to maintain good relationships and receive personal acceptance; motto is ''If you can't say something nice, don't say anything at all'' (s/a)	9	1
8. Views conflict as a win-lose situation or as a power struggle in which one person must fail so that the other can succeed; not possible to compromise (f/c)	1	9
9. Tries to find a solution that everyone can live with (c)	5	5
10. Views conflict as beneficial if handled in an open manner; lays all cards on the table (ps/c)	9	9
11. Feels little concern for people or production of results but has great desire for noninvolvement (w/a)	1	1
12. Views open conflict as destructive; gives in to the will of others if necessary (s/a)	9	1

	Concern for People	Concern for Production
13. Has great respect for power and submits to arbitration only because the arbitrator's power is greater (f/c)	1	9
14. Uses voting or other methods of compromise as a way to avoid direct confrontation; believes that a high-quality solution is not as important as a workable or agreeable solution (c)	5	5
15. Attempts to reach a consensus agreement; willing to spend a great deal of time and effort to achieve it (ps/c)	9	9
A. Total each column score =	_____	_____
B. Averages (column total divided by number of questions answered)	_____	_____

Now, plot your averages on the table in Figure 2.

If your average people-production scores were close to 1, 1, you prefer a "withdrawal/avoidance" (w/a) or "win–lose" conflict style.

If your average people-production scores were close to 9, 1, you prefer a "forcing" (f) or "win–lose" conflict style.

If your average people-production scores were close to 1, 9, you prefer a "problem-solving/collaboration" (ps/c) or "win–win" conflict style.

If your average people-production scores were close to 5, 5, you prefer a "compromising" (c) or "lose–lose" conflict style.

Are you locked in to a particular style? No. As with the communication styles quiz you took earlier, your goal should be to find out what style you naturally prefer and to

Figure 2. Conflict resolution styles.

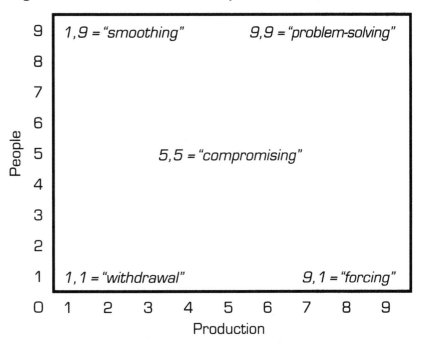

learn how to "flex" to another style as required by the people involved and the situation.

WHEN TO USE EACH OF THE FIVE STYLES OF CONFLICT RESOLUTION

When should you use or not use each of the styles?

Strategy #1: Withdrawal/Avoidance

Withdrawal/avoidance is a strategy that calls for ignoring conflict in the hope that it will go away. People who practice this style will maintain neutrality at all costs and views conflict as a worthless and punishing exercise. They will remove themselves physically or mentally from the situation and feel little concern for people and for task accomplishment but a great desire for noninvolvement.

Although you might think this is not an effective strategy, it is the best strategy to use:

- When the issues are trivial
- When the parties in a conflict lack conflict ("win-win") skills
- When the potential losses in the conflict outweigh the potential gains (based on a simple "cost-benefit" analysis of the situation)
- When there is not enough time to work through the issues of the conflict

What is the drawback to using withdrawal/avoidance? It only delays the confrontation!

Strategy #2: Smoothing/Accommodation

Adherents of this strategy feel a greater concern for people than for whether a task is completed, and they try to smooth over or ignore conflict to keep everybody happy. They see open conflict as destructive and will give in to the will of others if necessary to maintain the peace.

Smoothing or accommodation may be the best strategy to use:

- When the issues are minor
- When damage to the relationship will hurt all parties involved in a conflict
- When there is a need to temporarily reduce the level of conflict in order to get more information
- When tempers are too hot to progress

What is the drawback to using smoothing or accommodation? It offers a temporary solution only—sort of like putting a bandaid on a major wound.

Strategy #3: Compromise

Compromisers believe that everybody should have an equal chance to express opinions, often try to find a solution everybody can live with, like to use voting as a way of avoiding direct conflict, and believe that a high-quality solution is not as important as a solution everybody can live with.

When should you compromise?

- When both parties will gain something in the compromise
- When an ideal solution isn't needed
- When you need a temporary solution for a complex problem
- When both sides have equal power

Why isn't compromise the best method to use? Everybody loses something (that is the definition of compromise), and you probably won't reach the best solution through compromise.

Strategy #4: Forcing/Competition

People who prefer forcing or competition see reaching their own goals as more important than people and see nothing wrong with using force to get what they want. They see conflict as a win-lose situation in which their opponents must lose for them to win and have great respect for power. They submit to arbitration only when the arbitrator's power is greater than theirs.

When should you use a forcing or competitive style?

- When you or the group needs an immediate action or decision
- When all parties in a conflict expect and appreciate the use of power and force
- When all parties in a conflict understand and accept the power relationship between them

What are the drawbacks in using forcing or competition? The real cause of the conflict remains unresolved, and any solution achieved will only be temporary. You also have to consider the unmanaged emotions of the loser, who will probably seek revenge when he or she sees the opportunity.

Strategy #5: Problem Solving or Collaboration

People who follow a problem-solving or collaborative strategy give equal consideration to people and to results and view conflict as beneficial if handled in an open manner. Open and honest communication ("laying all one's cards on the table") is a key characteristic. They attempt to achieve a group consensus in solving the problem and are willing to spend a lot of time to do so.

When should you use problem solving or collaboration? These strategies are effective:

- When everybody in the conflict is trained in problem-solving methods
- When the parties have common goals
- When the conflict results from a simple misunderstanding or lack of communication

What are the drawbacks of using problem solving or collaboration? It will not work with people who have different values or goals. If somebody is determined to use power, for instance, all you can do is try to use a problem-solving orientation. But you may be forced to use another style.

Another drawback is that problem solving is a time-consuming practice. If the group or situation calls for a fast decision, you may have to use a forcing style.

HOW DO YOU USE A PROBLEM SOLVING (WIN-WIN) STRATEGY?

Do you put off solving problems and making decisions? Don't worry if you answered yes. Many of us hate to make decisions, and for a variety of reasons. Perhaps you put off

The reflective thinking process can be a powerful "win-win" negotiating tool.

decisions waiting for better, perfect data to come in (they rarely do). Maybe you hate to make a choice because somebody might get upset. Or perhaps you put off decision making because of bad experiences in the past. How many of us have tried to solve a problem within a group and wondered what good came out of all the fighting?

How can you as an individual or a member of a group make better decisions? The key is to use the *reflective thinking process,* a proven framework for solving problems.

The reflective thinking process can be a powerful "win-win" negotiating tool that will help empower everybody involved in a negotiation to learn to agree honestly about things that affect them. The result should be better, more effective decisions, with a high degree of buy-in.

Steps in the Reflective Thinking Process

1. Whether acting as an individual or part of a group, the first step is to *identify the problem.* If you're part of a group, this may take some open and honest discussion. Is what you've identified really the problem or merely a symptom of a problem? Does this problem identification satisfy your needs? Is the problem identification clear and concise? Can you write the problem on the back of a matchbook cover?

2. *Brainstorm* a list of possible solutions. This is an easy technique that anybody can use. Take out a sheet of paper (or use a flipchart, overhead, or blackboard so all can see). Write down all the possible solutions you or the group can think of. Do not allow any negative comments about ideas. You are going after a quantity of ideas, regardless of quality. The more ideas, the better. When you've run out of new ideas, you or the group should start to weed out clearly unworkable ideas until you get four or five solutions that you or the group can live with.

3. *Evaluate* alternative solutions. You can use a technique called force field analysis (see Figure 3). Take out an-

Figure 3. Force-field analysis.

Alternatives	(+) Positives	(−) Negatives
Solution 1		
Solution 2		
Solution 3		
Solution 4		
Solution 5		

other sheet of paper, draw a line down the middle, and head one column " + " and the other " − " (for benefits and risks). Then generate all the positives and negatives to each solution.

4. Now it's time to make a decision. There are three ways you can decide what alternative to use. One method is what most of us think of first when working in a group: vote. Voting is fast. But what about the people in a group that are on the losing end of the vote? These people can be powerful internal enemies to any decision made this way. A second possibility is consensus, the preferred method most of the time for group decision making. Consensus, or talking out the alternatives until everybody decides on a best solution, produces a decision with a high degree of member commitment. However, consensus does take time, lots of it. Ever served on a jury? If time is important, consensus may not be possible. The third method is a hybrid decision-making method sometimes called the nominal group technique (n.g.t.), in which all members involved in a problem individually rank order their preferences. Then the rankings are averaged. The group agrees ahead of time that the alterna-

tive that receives the highest average ranking will be the group decision. You should use n.g.t. when your group gets deadlocked. It's not as good as consensus but it's better than voting. A benefit of n.g.t. is that it yields a higher degree of commitment from group members than voting. A drawback of n.g.t. is that it is time-consuming, although not as much as consensus.

5. Set up a plan to *monitor the results* of the chosen solution. This is a crucial step in group decision making. The tendency for some groups, especially groups that fought during past decision-making sessions, is to skip this test. They are so often relieved that they made a decision without all the fighting and yelling they forget to do it! The group needs to do some anticipatory planning. How will the group monitor the result? Should it check every month, every quarter, every year? Who will do what when, where, and how? Make sure the group agrees ahead of time how to monitor the solution chosen. This bit of preplanning will save time and disagreement down the road.

This win-win (us against the problem) orientation is very effective for the vast majority of problems that confront you or your group. But there are some situations where the reflective thinking method may not be the best way to make decisions and solve problems. Imagine, for example, a navy battleship whose captain is a big believer in participate management and who regularly uses the reflective thinking model in solving problems aboard ship. The officers under the captain's command enjoy having a say in decisions that affect them and their sailors. And it's a good way for the captain to help develop the leadership skills of his officers. Then one day, the battleship strays into enemy waters and is torpedoed. The ship lists badly to the left, or port, side. Should the captain call the ship's officers together and follow the reflective thinking model in deciding what to do? Or does the situation and followers demand another kind of decision making? The captain could follow the reflective thinking model of decision making. Everybody on board would feel good about the process. But they would also probably drown. Perhaps both the captain and sailors aboard that ship would appreciate the captain's use of an authoritative decision-making method: "You radio for help! You lower the life boats! You break out the ammunition!"

Reflective thinking is a process that, by and large, produces high-quality decisions that everybody can support. But sometimes an authoritarian decision-making style is preferable. It depends on the negotiating situation and on the maturity level (knowledge, prior history, motivation) of the people involved.

If used improperly, the reflective thinking process can make you appear indecisive. More than three-quarters of the decisions most of us have to make can and should be made on the spot, perhaps 15 percent need some time and thought, and 5 percent of the decisions shouldn't have to be made at all.

Think of the navy captain. The sailors under the captain's command might see the use of reflective thinking in a crisis situation as a sign that he is indecisive and weak. If the other side knew that the captain always made decisions that way, they would also think him weak. Decisiveness in some situations inspires support and can intimidate the opposition. In competitive circumstances, the not-so-hot decision made quickly can yield better results than a good decision made slowly. As the management expert Peter Drucker says, "People who don't take risks generally make about two big mistakes a year. People who do take risks generally make about two big mistakes a year."

Research has proved that the greater rewards go to those who take more (calculated) risks.

CHAPTER REVIEW

1. Can conflict ever be good? Why or why not?

_____

_____

2. How do you naturally handle conflict? Which one of the five styles is closest to your style?

   _____

   _____

3. Why should you first try for a win-win agreement?

   _____

   _____

CHAPTER 4

THE IMPORTANCE OF ASSERTIVENESS IN NEGOTIATIONS

How can you better handle personal conflict situations? What's the best way to handle difficult people? The first step is to learn to be more assertive.

People characteristically deal with others in one of four ways:

Passive			Aggressive
Nonassertive	**Indirect**	**Assertive**	**Agressive**
Passive wimp; doormat	**Manipulative weasel**	**Win-win team player**	**Mean bully**
Self-denying, placating, submissive, avoiding; soft voice; downcast eyes	Sneaky, coy, seductive, vindictive, revengeful; chooses for others	Stands up for own rights while respecting others'; makes own choices	Denies others' rights; dominating; demanding; judgmental; chooses for others

Why should you try to be assertive? Have you ever gotten what you want by being passive? Most likely not.

QUIZ: HOW ASSERTIVE ARE YOU?

Respond to each item with a yes or no. Then check your score with the key at the end of the quiz. This quiz will let you know if you need to work on being more assertive.

1. I state my own view when someone with more authority disagrees with me.
2. I express irritation if someone with whom I am talking starts talking to someone else in the middle of our conversation.
3. I insist that the landlord or repairperson make timely repairs.
4. I openly express love and affection and tell people that I care for them.
5. I make direct eye contact when speaking with others.
6. When a person is being highly unfair, I call it to his or her attention.
7. I ask friends for small favors or help.
8. I say no without apology if people make unreasonable demands of me.
9. At work, I suggest new procedures or ways of doing things.
10. I cut short telephone calls when I am busy.
11. I am able to refuse unreasonable requests made by others.
12. I look for a seat in the front of a crowded room rather than stand in the back.
13. If someone keeps kicking the back of my chair, I ask him or her to stop.
14. I can speak in front of a group without becoming overly anxious.
15. I have confidence in my own judgment.
16. I seek repayment from a friend who borrowed $10 and has forgotten to repay me.
17. I can stay calm when others are scrutinizing my work or reviewing it.
18. I speak up in a meeting if I feel that my idea is relevant.
19. I do not apologize for what I am about to say.
20. I ask a friend who keeps calling me very late at night not to call after a certain time.
21. When merchandise is faulty, I return it for adjustment.
22. I can ask for a raise or promotion without feeling overly anxious.
23. I speak firmly and loudly enough to be heard and understood.
24. I state my own and others' limitations without feeling guilty.

25. When I meet someone for the first time, I introduce myself and extend my hand.
26. I can work with others without trying to make them feel guilty or manipulated.
27. I express my opinions rather than keeping them to myself.
28. In a restaurant, if my meal is unacceptable, I ask the waiter to correct it.
29. I am able to confront an issue or problem at work rather than call in sick.
30. I insist that my spouse or roommate take on a fair share of the household chores.

Total YES _____   Total NO _____

Scoring Key: *22 or more yes responses = You're assertive enough*
15–21 yes responses = You have some areas to work on
Fewer than 22 yes responses = You're the mayor of Wimp City!

Once you know you're assertive enough—that you stand up for your rights, are diplomatic, and have a win–win problem-solving orientation—you can use a variety of tactics to handle difficult people and situations.

How do you know you should confront a problem? You need to face up to a problem when:

1. A person's performance hinders achievement of your group goals. If a person's disruptive behavior affects your group's work, you know it's time to take action.
2. You find out that a person's actions will affect adversely your own success. When a person does something that might cause you harm, you have to ask yourself, "Can I afford to ignore this?"
3. A problem keeps sticking its head up and causing you problems every time you see it. You may fear that bringing up a problem will open a Pandora's box of other troubles. But remember, by doing nothing, you'll probably only make matters worse.

Before confronting another person, make sure you aren't contributing to the problem.

Before confronting another person, make sure you aren't contributing to the problem. What part of the situation might you be contributing to? What can you do about it?

SIX WAYS TO HANDLE CONFLICT

#1: Gentle Confrontation

This technique calls for openly confronting the situation in a diplomatic manner.

How do you know when you're successful at gentle confrontation? You should be able to answer yes to all three of these questions: Has the other person's behavior changed? Have you preserved the self-esteem of the other person? Have you preserved the relationship?

Here's how to prepare for gentle confrontation:

- Maintain control of your emotions. Avoid overreacting.
- Don't complain. Endless complaining about somebody's behavior will accomplish nothing. You'll probably divide people by complaining. People will end up choosing sides, yours or the other person's. In addition, by complaining, you'll hurt your credibility. Complaining or whining makes it easy for others simply to tune you out. One of the quickest ways to gain the mistrust and resentment of people around you is to complain to one of them about one of their peers.
- Rehearse what you'll say.
- Make sure you're aware and in control of your voice, body, and facial expression.
- Don't lecture. Nothing turns people off more than being talked down to, lecture-style.
- Be willing to listen; don't interrupt.

There are five elements to constructive *assertive confrontation:*

1. Objectively describe the undersirable behavior you're trying to change. Do not be subjective; do not be personal.
2. Listen to the other person's response.

3. Identify the specific tangible effects the behavior has on your team in terms of cost, time, or money.

4. Describe your future expectations in specific terms.

5. Gain commitment or agreement from the other person. You can either ask him if he agrees, or you can say, "This seems like a reasonable request, doesn't it?" While you're saying this, physically nod up and down, look the other person in the eye, and look for agreement. You'll find it is hard to shake your head no when somebody you're talking to is shaking hers yes.

Most people want to be reason-able.

Most people want to be reasonable. Getting the other side to agree that you are being reasonable can be a powerful tool in resolving conflict. It can move the other side to show reasonableness as well, and that may mean a bigger concession to you in the future.

Now tackle this case study:

Your team is negotiating to buy a large allotment of jet fuel. Jerry, one of the sellers, has raised and lowered the price of the fuel several times without explanation.

How do you handle this situation using the assertive confrontation model?

Hint: Be polite, be specific, describe the effects of her behavior on you, ask for something specific, ask for commitment.

Do you often find yourself saying yes to a request when you really want to say no? Do you find that people always ask you favors because you're the path of least resistance? If so, you need to be assertive—to stand up for your rights, manage your time and tasks, and say no.

Using the principles of assertive confrontation, how would you say no to the following cases?

1. You refuse the other side's demand for an extended warranty on the framing implements you're trying to sell, since such a practice is not followed in your industry.

Hint: Explain that your boss would never agree to such a demand. Second, offer an alternative (people are more likely to agree with you if you offer them an alternative). Perhaps you could extend such an unprecedented warranty if the other side locks in to a longer-term contract. Third, ask for commitment and understanding. The wrong way to respond is to say, "I said no. What part of no don't you understand?" Put yourself on the receiving end of that message. How would it make you feel? Keep in mind that you want to say no but at the same time preserve the relationship.

2. How about saying no to a boss? Your team leader has just asked you to stay late again to work on a proposal that is due. You refuse.

Hint: State, "I understand that the proposal is important. As you know, I've stayed late three nights in a row to work on this. But tonight I have important family business I must attend to. However, I'd be glad to come in a half hour early tomorrow to work on the project. Doesn't that seem fair to you?"

Gentle confrontation is also useful in combating the grapevine, that fast and often accurate (some experts say that it is accurate three quarters of the time!) organizational communication channel we've all used. You can waste a lot of time trying to stamp out the grapevine, but it just won't go away.

The rumors it spreads can lower morale and be quite disruptive.

How can you take advantage of the grapevine?

- You can selectively work the grapevine. If you have important information to get out, know that the fastest way to get it out is through the "vine." Then follow up the news with the official announcement.
- If the grapevine carries inaccurate rumors, try to wait it out. Maybe the rumor will run its course.
- If the rumor continues, make it news. Talk about the rumor, and deny it.
- Ridicule the rumor. Call it preposterous. People might then ridicule the rumor mongers.
- Try making a full disclosure of the facts. This is the best way to fight a rumor and can often stop a rumor before it even gets started.

#2: Disarming the Opposition

Sometimes the other person has a legitimate beef against you. If you deny reality, the other person will be angry and the problem will persist. By acknowledging that the other person is right, you're going to go a long way to solve the crisis.

Let's assume that a police officer pulls you over for speeding (yes, you were driving a little fast):

Usual Defensive Approach:

You: What's the problem? I wasn't speeding. My friend sitting right here will vouch for me.
Police officer: Don't tell me that. My speedometer doesn't lie.

How would you disarm the opposition?

_____

_____

What might the officer say?

_____

_____

Hint: Surprise the officer. He expects you to deny that you were speeding. Admit it. As Henry Ford II was fond of saying, "Never complain, never explain."

You can use the same technique while negotiating. Just don't overdo it; if you get predictable, you'll lose effectiveness.

#3: Handling Anger

Never tell another person, "Don't be angry." Instead, encourage the person to tell you all about what's angering her.

There are five things to do with an angry person:

1. Listen. Maybe the person has a right to be angry.
2. Don't argue, even if that is what the person wants. A person's feelings are neither right nor wrong. Perhaps the other person's self-esteem is in the dumpster. Compliment him whenever possible.
3. Find out why the person is angry. Ask open-ended questions, not yes-no questions.
4. Show empathy. Use the reflective listening technique of occasionally paraphrasing the other person's words.
5. If you're in the wrong, admit it!

There are four techniques you can use to prevent blowups:

1. When you criticize others, concentrate on observed behavior, not the person. Keep it specific and not personal.
2. Avoid embarrassing or demeaning the person, especially in front of others.
3. Don't blame unless you have to and you are 100 percent sure you're right.

4. Encourage cheerfulness, and use light humor whenever possible.

If you feel you're in danger of really exploding in anger, consider these suggestions:

- Go for a walk by yourself to get away from the problem for a while. Sometimes it clears the way for more constructive thinking.
- Write an angry letter. Just don't send it. This gets the anger out of your system without hurting anybody.
- Then write a second, calmer, more rational letter. Either send it to the person that angers you or use the writing of the letter as a rehearsal for facing the individual in person.

Blue Cross and Blue Shield of Michigan proposes twelve guidelines that you should remember the next time you have to tell someone that she has done something wrong:

1. Identify the behavior that you want to criticize. Direct your criticism at action, not the person.
2. Make criticisms specific. Not "You always miss deadlines" but "You missed the March 15 deadline for your report."
3. Be sure the behavior you're criticizing can be changed. Foreign accents, baldness, and other things tangentially related to some business dealings cannot always be changed.
4. Use "I" and "we" to stress that you want to work out the problem together, rather than making threats.
5. Make sure that the other person understands the reason for your criticism.
6. Don't belabor the point. Make it short and sweet; no lectures.
7. Offer incentives for changed behavior. Offer to help the person correct the problem.
8. Don't set a tone of anger or sarcasm. Both are counterproductive.
9. Show the person you understand his feelings.

10. If you're putting your criticism in writing, cool off before writing the critical letter or memo. Be sure only the person it is intended for sees it.
11. Start off by saying something good.
12. At the end, reaffirm your support for and confidence in the person.

What should you do if the rational approach doesn't work? Sometimes, you can use a good old-fashioned temper tantrum to focus people's attention on a problem. This works best if you have a reputation for being a rational, cool customer. Do it only to get people's attention on a problem, be selective about using this drastic measure (if you overuse it, you'll just be seen as a hothead), don't make it personal, and aim your anger at the situation, not at a person.

Here's a case study:

I've got to straighten out a problem with somebody from the other side, and I'm sure I'll get angry. And that's going to cause more trouble. What should I do?

_____

_____

Hint: Let the person know you're angry. Be specific about describing what you think is wrong. Stick to talking about actions and behaviors, not about attitudes or motivation. Listen. Look for solutions to the problem so that everybody wins. You can influence and persuade others by not yelling and by remaining in control.

#4: Appeal to a Powerful Third Party

Sometimes a gentle approach to a problem doesn't work. The other person may not want to compromise or find a win-win solution to the conflict. He may want to use power to solve the conflict. In that case, you may have to do the same. Use this tactic only when winning is *very* important, because it will certainly create ill will.

One example of an appeal to a powerful third party is a labor dispute that you take to your state labor board or union. The third party will impose a settlement that will probably please neither side.

#5: Exchange Images With the Antagonist

To use this strategy, tell the other person that you understand her point of view. On a piece of paper, write down your side of the dispute and what you think the other person's side is. The other person does the same for you. Then you exchange the written images and discuss them.

#6: Interpret the Other Person's Game

How do you handle another person's game playing? One way to handle this is to confront the person with your interpretation of what is going on.

The tactic is called Now I've Got You, you S.O.B.

Let's say you find out that a "friend" has been bad mouthing you to the press. Instead of slugging the person, face him and in your best business tone say, "I'm very much aware that you're saying these things about me to the press. We have to find a way to make this stop. If you've got a problem with me, deal with me directly."

The other person will probably be shocked and try to deny what he's been doing. At that point, just repeat what you said in as businesslike a tone as possible.

If the behavior happens again, march up to the person, look him in the eye, tell him that you know what he's doing, and ask him to stop (you can even point your finger). You want to be as firm and as serious as possible.

Game players hate to be caught. If you keep confronting them, chances are they'll eventually decide you're too much of a hassle to pick on and move to some other victim.

CHAPTER REVIEW

To find out what you have learned so far, take the following open book review quiz.

1. Can conflict ever be good?

   _____

2. How do you handle conflict?

   _____

   _____

3. What are the three kinds of conflict resolution? What is the win-win outcome? Why is it normally the preferable outcome?

   _____

   _____

   _____

4. Why is assertiveness preferable to any other way of dealing with others?

   _____

5. How would you gently confront a problem person?

   _____

   _____

6. How should you deal with anger?

   _____

   _____

7. What should you do about temper tantrums?

   _____

CHAPTER 5

GETTING DOWN TO BUSINESS: LET'S NEGOTIATE!

Almost everything we do involves some kind of negotiation. Conflicts in business and in personal life are commonly solved through negotiations. When we buy things, sell ideas or solve problems, negotiation gets us what we want. But most people are uncomfortable with negotiations (remember the last time you bought a new car?). In reality, there's nothing sinister about being a good negotiator. It requires nothing more than common sense and communication. Negotiation is a way to get your fair share, whether it's selling a proposal to your boss, settling a labot dispute, buying real estate, or getting that new car. The reason we avoid negotiation situations is because we've handled them poorly in the past, "giving away the farm" just to settle.

You already probably have these skills:

- *Thinking on your feet.* Impromptu speaking situations are excellent practice for negotiating. Can you respond quickly and intelligently with only moments' notice?
- *Planning and organizing.* These skills are important for speech success and are crucial in negotiations.
- *Listening.* Listening means comprehending, not just hearing. Do you understand what others are saying? Can you "read" what they want? Negotiators are the best listeners.

You can master your life through knowing:

1. The kinds of "games" people are likely to play while negotiating.

2. How to control the four crucial negotiating variables—power, time, information, and the context of negotiations.
3. Useful strategies and tactics for increasing your negotiating chances.

When two sides can't agree on an issue, they have three options: They can do nothing ("Oh well, I tried. He just won't listen!"), one side can force a solution ("You'll do it because I'm the boss!"), or they can reach a mutually satisfying agreement through negotiations.

FIRST THINGS FIRST: PREPARE TO NEGOTIATE

In negotiations, as in most things in life, you can never be too prepared. Answer the following questions, taken from Marvin Gottleib and William J. Healy's book *Making Deals,* to make sure you're ready:

1. *When is the negotiation taking place?* Are there fluctuations in the business cycle, demands on cash flow, or anything else that might affect a deal?

_____

2. *How much time do you have?*

_____

3. *What are the issues to be negotiated?* An issue is anything that has value to either side.

_____

_____

4. *What issues should you avoid?* Never bring up anything where you have a weak position.

_____

_____

5. *How should issues be ranked?* Rate the importance of your issues by dividing them into three categories: *need to have* (you won't consider a deal without them), *nice to have* (you'll work hard to get them), and *tradeoff* (what you can bargain away).

Your Issues

1. *My Need to Haves:*

2. *My Nice to Haves:*

3. *My Tradeoffs:*

Your Opponent's Issues★

1. *Need to Haves:*

2. *Nice to Haves:*

3. *Their Tradeoffs:*

★Based on your research and best guesses.

Next, consider these points:

1. *What are your limits?* Do you have the authority to make a deal? Try to enter the negotiations with the highest amount of authority possible because it will give you confidence. Don't, on the other hand, admit that you have absolute authority because you want to be able to say (if you need to) that you need to consult the ''higher-ups.''

---

2. *What are the facts?* The more you know about the other side and the deal, the more effective you will be. Always ask questions!

---

3. *What is the other side's point of view?* Anticipate the other side's position. How do their people see you? What is important to them? How badly do they need this deal? This is key: Can they walk away from the negotiations?

---

4. *What do you know about the other negotiators?* Understand their beliefs, attitudes, styles.

_____

5. *What outside influences affect the negotiations?* Know about things like current market conditions, relevant laws and regulations, competitor actions, component and labor shortages or surpluses, political influences, union relations, even if possible, personal problems of the negotiators.

_____

6. *What will you accept?* Know what your best possible deal would be. Also, know the minimum terms you will accept.

_____

_____

7. *What's your plan of action?* Write up an agenda that includes what you'd like to discuss first, second, third, and last. Pre-plan. Avoid agreeing to too many minor issues at the beginning. The value of these seemingly minor issues may increase as the negotiations go on. You can also use a minor (to you) issue as a concession to the other side, giving up little or nothing in exchange for something.

_____

_____

THE RITUAL OF NEGOTIATING: THE SIX BASIC STEPS

Negotiating is like a ritual or a long dance that must have its steps done in the right order. The ritual of negotiating has six steps:

1. Getting to know each other
2. Setting goals and objectives

3. Beginning negotiations
4. Expressing disagreement and conflict
5. Reassessing and compromising
6. Reaching agreement

1. *Getting to know each other.* Although the temptation is to jump right into negotiations, it is important for negotiators to spend some time getting to know each other. Remember what you've learned about listening. It is during this period that you'll have a chance to see what is important to the other side and to assess the individual personalities of the people involved. Furthermore, by spending some time getting to know each other, you'll both be investing energy in the process. Have you ever noticed how difficult it is to end negotiations once you've gotten to know the other side?

Agreement is the ultimate objective of negotiating.

Since agreement is the ultimate objective of negotiating, make sure you're negotiating with people who can make decisions. Some parties will negotiate to determine your position and then tell you they don't have the authority to accept your terms. They'll then go to another person (their boss, some "higher-up") who will reject what you've negotiated as a ploy to try to get a better deal.

2. *Setting goals and objectives.* Negotiations should then flow into a general statement of goals and objectives. There is no need to raise specific issues here because both sides are starting to get to know each other. Try starting off with a good general positive statement such as "I'd like to make sure this works in a way that will help everybody." Then listen to see what the other side says. Does it agree on a win-win scenario? If it appears it will be playing lose-lose or lose-win, all is not lost. But this is the first place where you'll find out if there are any differences in goals.

3. *Beginning negotiations.* Some negotiations are easy; some are very complex. You won't know the direction the negotiations are going to take until you've shared goals and objectives with the other side. The other side may have hidden needs that may not come out until later in the process. Issues may be bundled together ("I won't do X unless you

do Y") or separated ("Let's have separate negotiations for X and Y"). If you've done your homework, you will have already decided where the advantage lies for you on bundling or separating issues.

There is disagreement on whether to try to begin negotiations with a minor issue or a major issue. Some say that settling a minor issue first creates goodwill that can last throughout the negotiations; others say you're better off settling a major issue first, especially if failing to reach agreement on the major issue would make the minor issues moot.

4. *Expressing disagreement and conflict.* Once you've defined the issues, disagreement and conflict often occur. Remember, information comes out of conflict. It needn't scare you. You should expect and welcome this phase of negotiations. Handling conflict effectively will bring the parties together; handling it poorly will divide the parties even further. When presenting issues, most negotiators say what they "want." It is your job to find out what they "need" or will settle for. Few negotiators get everything they want. It might be in your best interest sometimes to compromise or modify the goals you had coming in to the session. Remember, you should see conflict not as a test of power but as a chance to find out what people need.

5. *Reassessing and Compromising.* At some point during the negotiations, somebody may move toward compromise. If you hear statements that begin "Suppose that . . . ?" or "What if . . . ?" or "How would you feel about . . . ?," listen closely; the other side may be hinting at a move closer to your position. Don't try to pin the other side down quickly, because this could cause the other side to withdraw.

When responding to statements of goals, positions, and offers, it's a good idea to use the reflective listening technique. If the other side offers to sell your car for $2,000, you should say, "So you're offering this auto to me for $2,000?" If you use this technique:

- The other side may improve the offer because it thinks your response is a negative.
- The other side may try to justify its position. This

will provide you with opportunities to challenge its
assumptions.

- You will gain time to think about a counteroffer. If
  the other side repeats your counteroffer, confirm it;
  don't sweeten it. This forces the other side to accept
  it, reject it, or suggest an alternative.

6. *Reaching agreement.* At this stage you settle on an
agreement. It's best to do this in writing. Volunteer to do
the contract writing. This gives you tremendous power. As
you go along in the negotiations, take notes and settle on a
lot of little agreements. Let the other side know you're
keeping track of the little agreements. You can even provide
copies of all the little agreements you both have made to
the other side. Make sure you have an agreement that gives
everyone an incentive to comply with the agreement. There
should also be negative consequences for noncompliance.
Document the agreement and obtain sign-offs by decision
makers. Then stay in touch with the other party while the
agreement is implemented.

CREATING A WIN-WIN SITUATION

To be a great win-win negotiator, you must be able to use
four essential variables—time, power, information, and context.

1. *Time.* The time you choose to negotiate is of great
importance. Unfortunately, what gets done in this world
usually gets done right before deadline. If you understand
that negotiation takes place over time and is an ongoing
process, you won't feel compelled to rush a decision. The
person who feels under the gun is more likely to give something up to complete a deal. People set up time limits in
negotiations. Try not to interfere with the deadlines of others, but never let your opponent know your deadline.

How might you know that the people on the other side
are getting close to their deadline? Look for the following
clues:

- They pick up the pace of discussion.
- They suddenly soften an earlier hard-line position.
- They become preoccupied with how much time has passed (a lot of glancing at watches?).
- A new person suddenly enters the negotiation.
- They concede an issue.

When it serves your purposes, you can create time pressure on the other side to move discussion along or to resolve a deadlock. Try:

- Letting the other side think that your supply of what it wants is limited
- Referring to an imminent price increase
- Making a limited-time offer
- Making an offer contingent on an immediate response

Be wary of creating a false deadline. A skilled opponent can call your bluff by ignoring it. Once the deadline passes, you'll lose your credibility.

80 percent of the concessions tend to be made during the last 20 percent of the negotiating session.

A strong argument for keeping as many concessions as possible until the end is the 80/20 rule: 80 percent of the concessions tend to be made during the last 20 percent of the negotiating session. A concession that means little to the other side in the early going may be just the thing to close the deal. However, you still should carefully consider using a small concession early to begin negotiations on a positive footing.

Another thing to consider is how to time your moves. You've probably heard the old saying "Timing is everything." It is. When is the best time to negotiate a deal on an automobile? Probably at season's end or when you know the dealer really must make deals (perhaps it is going out of business or faces pressure to reduce inventory).

What time constraints do you face?

How will you hide your time deadlines?

_____

What do you need to look for from the other side to see if it is pressured by time?

_____

Are there any timing considerations that could help you make a better deal?

_____

2. *Power.* Far too many negotiators play the win-lose game because they're afraid of losing. They view negotiation as a threat to their power, so their aim is always to have the other guy lose. But the only way you really lose is if you let the other side win without getting anything for yourself. Build a win-win climate by being open and honest about what you want. Explain why something is unacceptable. Appeal to the other side's sense of fairness.

The real key to power is perception. If the other side thinks you have power, you do. If you think you have power, it's far easier to convince the other side that you have it. If you think the other side has power, it does. You can, however, diminish the other side's power by simply refusing to acknowledge it!

Other ways to gain the power edge include:

- *Establish legitimacy based on a demonstrated need.* Legitimate power comes from a job title or formal position. Also, understand the power of written proposals, which give an aura of legitimacy merely by being printed.
- *Don't fear risks.* Calculated risk takers often end up with respect, higher rewards, and the most power. If you go into a negotiation believing you can walk out if you don't get what you need, you have power. You can give yourself walk-out power by always having alternatives. Never ever go into a negotiating session

with only one choice. Fall in love with three. Love three houses, three cars, three things (but not three spouses!)

- *Be persistent.* Ask for what you want several times in a negotiating session.
- *Personalize yourself.* Make the other side see you as a person and not as just a mouthpiece for your company. Let it know you have feelings, problems, and concerns just as it does. Instead of dealing for the company, deal for yourself.
- *Acknowledge your limitations.* Don't be afraid to say "I don't know," "I don't understand," or "Can you help me?" now and then. Done at the right times, such admissions project a sense of humanness without suggesting weakness. They reinforce the problem-solving climate.

You might also have reward or punishment power. This type of power often lies with the buyer in sales negotiations, although buyers are also subject to rewards and punishments. How would the buyer's boss, for example, react if the deal were to fall through?

You or your opponent may also have identification power. This power comes not from position but from your relationship with other, powerful people in the organization and from how these people view you. Have you ever known people in your organization who wielded power beyond their position? Was it because they were well liked or well connected?

What power sources do you presently have?

What sources of power can you get?

What is the key to power?

---

3. *Information.* The more information you have, the better. Know your opponent's background (expertise, experience in negotiations, goals) and personal characteristics (emotional and personal needs, involvement in office politics). Also find out how much your opponent wants what he or she is fighting for. The more a person wants something, the more likely that person will make concessions. Try to increase the other side's desire for what you can offer in negotiation. On the other hand, don't reveal how much you want what it has. The instant you show how much you need or want something, you lose negotiating power.

What sources of information do you need to tap on your opponent?

4. *Context.* A vital variable in negotiation is the context of the negotiations. You can often make superb one-time deals based on context. For example, a company buys the house of a transferred employee. The company is not in the business of buying and selling houses and wants to move the house as soon as possible. This creates a favorable situation for a potential buyer trying to negotiate a purchase.

If there's a chance at a long-term relationship, don't jump in and try to make a killing even if the context is favorable to one. Always ask yourself how the present deal might affect future relations.

What is there about the context of the negotiations that can help or hurt you?

RESPONDING TO NEGOTIATING PLOYS

Now that you know the basics of negotiating—the types of games people play (and why win-win is the best outcome) and the four most important variables in every negotiation (time, power, information, and context)—it's time to apply your strategies and tactics to the negotiator's table. Although win-win negotiations are becoming the norm, you're still going to run into folks who have succeeded through old-school hard bargaining. Your best defense against such people is to know the tactics they'll use and how to counteract them.

In preparation, develop an approach that is only a preliminary plan. Locking yourself into an inflexible plan will spell disaster when conditions change during the negotiations. Tactics vary according to the subject being negotiated and the people involved. Here are some proven techniques:

• Sometimes hard bargainers take an unreasonable opening position, hoping to force you to lower your expectations. An unprepared negotiator may panic and make early concessions. When faced with an extreme demand, restate it in your own words in terms more acceptable to you. Don't counter with your own list of unreasonable demands. You should, however, ask for more than you expect. This will give you some negotiating room. If you start off with a bottom offer, you'll have no more room to maneuver. How much more should you ask for? Try bracketing. If you want to pay $75,000 for a house and the seller asks for $80,000, try offering $70,000. You leave room for negotiating a win-win agreement.

• One tactic that works when you think you're being taken advantage of is to say you've changed your mind. The other side must either then make concessions or risk losing the whole argument.

• Remember to flinch in reaction to the other side's proposal. This little nonverbal signal may get the other side to lower its position. If you don't flinch, the other side may become more inflexible. It may think you're close to agreeing to its proposal.

• The other side may try the "limited authority" tactic. This is usually revealed in statements like "It's not up to me" or "I'd have to check with the people upstairs." The way to counter this is to make sure early on that you are actually dealing with a decision maker. If pushed, the other side may suddenly find the lost authority. Don't give in to save the deal. It shows weakness and you'll no doubt end up with a deal that you don't like.

• One tactic designed to undercut your feeling of power and to lower your expectations is the "take it or leave it" ploy. Again, a bad deal for you will be a bad deal for the other side, too. Restate your position and its benefits to the other side. Let the other side know that its offer is unworkable and unacceptable as it now stands.

When faced with temper tantrums, remain calm.

• When faced with temper tantrums, remain calm. Coolly ask for an explanation, and try to push the situation back into the win-win mode.

• If there's nothing more to negotiate or you're not getting what you want, you may have to walk out. The other side may be willing to make concessions if the negotiations are really important to them. This tactic can be risky. If the other side walks out, let it be the first to come back. This will give you the psychological edge of knowing how much it wants what you have.

• The "salami slice" tactic gives you what you want a little at a time rather than in one giant step. This strategy is said to have come from Matyas Rakosis, the general secretary of the Hungarian Communist Party, who explained it this way: "When you want to get hold of a salami which your opponents are strenuously defending, you must not grab at it. You must start by carving yourself a very thin slice. The owner of the salami will hardly notice it, or at least he will not mind very much. The next day you will carve another slice, then still another. And so, little by little, the salami will pass into your possession."

• There is something to be said for solving easy issues first and leaving the hard issues for last. However, making small concessions early can be a waste, because a small concession may be more valuable later in the negotiations. Remember, most things get done close to the deadline.

• Offer alternatives or proposals as "what ifs." This gives you information on how the other side might react and allows both sides to consider an issue without deciding on it.

• "Mutt 'n' Jeff" (or good guy/bad guy) tactics involve having the other side bring in a person you've never seen before (usually the bad guy) to tear your offer to pieces, make unreasonable demands, and storm out of the room. Then the original negotiator, the good guy, comes in and makes what seems to be reasonable requests. Their plan is to get you to make concessions that the good guy can sell to the bad guy. The way you counter this is to go back to your original plan during a recess; do not make concessions. You might even try using your own bad guy. But once you see the other side try this, assume that everybody is a bad guy.

• This point is controversial, but worth mentioning: Sometimes being the first to concede something gives you power. It gives the impression that you're the fair guy, and the other side may feel obligated to concede something in turn. Of course, you shouldn't give up something that's vital to you.

• If you need to concede a point, don't do it easily. Make your opponent work for it. There's truth to the saying "You'll appreciate it more if you work for it."

• One tactic that works when you think you're being taken advantage of is to say you've changed your mind. The other side will then make concessions; it's either that or risk losing the whole argument.

• Sometimes you'll find the other side talking as if you've agreed to a point that has never been discussed. This is called the "fait accompli" ("the thing is done"). The best defense again is to listen. If you catch the other side using this tactic, point it out. You can also appeal to the other side's "higher authority."

• The other side might also try a "standard practice" ploy. For instance, it may give you a contract and tell you it is standard practice. The assumption is that no one would want to change the contract because it is "standard."

• Your opponents may try the "phony issue" or "Trojan horse" tactic, making a big deal over one issue in the deal. By raising a ruckus over an issue that in reality may be minor to them, they hope to extract greater concessions from you. If the other side is making an issue out of price, perhaps the real issue is service; if the focus is on financing, the main concern may be delivery. Counter this by doing your research. Listen to the other side. Act skeptical.

• The "last-minute grab" (or nibble) is an attempt to get a last-minute concession from you. Timing is crucial here because this tactic is usually used near the end of negotiations when the parties are least likely to walk away from the table.

What tactics might your opponent use on you? How will you counter?

_____

_____

What tactics can you use? How will you use them?

_____

_____

COMMON MISTAKES TO AVOID

Research on negotiations and negotiators has found that the following are the most common kinds of mistakes negotiators make. How many of these mistakes have you made?

• *Being inadequately prepared.* Like anything else in life, you have to be prepared. Do you know what you want and need? Do you know what you can give up? Do you know the same about your opponent?

• *Winning at any cost.* This kind of error is fed by a number of psychological factors. Commitment to a course of action often biases your perception and judgment. You'll look for evidence to support your viewpoint and throw out information to the contrary. Always seek out information, good or bad, to counteract this problem. Stubborn commitment to one course of action may cause the negotiators to escalate into a win-lose or lose-lose battle. The use of intimidating (lose-lose or win-lose) behavior and a lack of self-control often cost time. Research shows that the tougher the tactics, the tougher the resistance. Persuasion, not dominance, makes for a better outcome.

• *Ignoring the natural give-and-take of win-win negotiations.* Remember, each side has to come away thinking it's gained something. This is especially important in cementing long-term relationships.

• *Failing to properly "frame" options in negotiations.* Make sure you state your terms or proposal in positive terms. For example, tell the other side, "Our wage proposal of $12 an hour is $2 more than you get now," rather than saying, "I know you wanted $15 an hour, but $12 an hour is the best I can do." A negative slant can cause the other side to make fewer concessions and may lead to an impasse.

• *Relying too much on public information.* Some negotiators rely too much on readily available information. Always ask how reliable the public information is. Go beyond the surface information. For instance, a good car salesman can make quite a case for an extended warranty. Who wouldn't want protection against costly repairs? But digging deeper, you might find that the extended warranty may partially duplicate the manufacturer's warranty and may cover only some cheap parts. You should have asked, "Is the warranty worth its cost?"

• *Experiencing the Winner's Curse.* This is the uneasy feeling you've been taken. Let's say you make a $7,000 offer on a car you know to be worth between $10,000 and $12,000. The seller quickly accepts your offer. How do you feel? You might feel pretty good at first; then you start to get the feeling that the seller knows something you don't. In a case like this, it might be a good thing to get advice from a trusted outsider. The point is to fight the tendency to ignore valuable information you could have learned simply by thinking about the other side's viewpoint.

• *Being overconfident.* Making many of the mistakes I've listed here can overinflate your confidence level and cloud your judgment. Overconfidence makes you disregard information that contradicts what you believe. How do you guard against overconfidence? Know that it can be a problem for you. Seek feedback from others about your pre-sumptions, ask yourself why you might be wrong, and know you're probably the most overconfident when you have the least amount of information.

WHEN WIN-WIN FAILS

Sometimes it isn't possible to achieve a win–win negotiating outcome. There may be a fundamental disagreement over the facts, or both sides may have opposing belief systems.

Don't give up. There are two other ways to settle really difficult disputes: *arbitration* and *mediation*.

There are two other ways to settle really difficult disputes: *arbitration* and *mediation*.

Arbitration is the use of an impartial third party to hear both sides of a dispute and to render a decision, which is usually binding. It may be helpful when both sides can't or won't budge from their positions, despite a lot of clear communication and when there is pressure to make a decision.

If the arbitrator's decision is not binding, the final step is litigation through the courts. And what happens in court? It's one side against the other: win–lose or, possibly, lose-lose.

Mediation is the attempt by an impartial third party to help the two sides in a dispute to communicate, negotiate, and reach agreement. Unlike an arbitrator, the mediator does not decide the outcome. Mediation is usually voluntary and nonbinding.

NEGOTIATING INTERNATIONALLY

The skills and techniques we use in successful win–win ne-gotiating in the United States may not work as well when we try to negotiate internationally.

One of the keys to successful international negotiating is to be aware of how people from other cultures perceive you. The minute you walk into a room full of people from another culture, you are stereotyped. Whether the stereotype is right or wrong is beside the point. It happens, and you have to be aware of it. Other people's perception of you affects the negotiations; so does your perception of them. It's therefore a good idea to know how Americans are often seen by their counterparts in other countries.

Probably the best piece of advice for dealing with people from other cultures is to try to surprise them by confounding their stereotype of you early on. You should do this by knowing some things about their country and their culture. Most non-Americans see Americans as geographically and culturally illiterate, and with good reason. Before you begin negotiating, therefore pull out an atlas. Look up the negotiators' country and study the oceans, mountain ranges, and city names. Read a little bit about the region. Then, armed with a little knowledge, you can ask intelligent questions about their homeland.

In addition, most non-English speakers think Americans know only English. Surprise them by knowing a few words of their language, such as the equivalent of *hello, goodbye,* and *how are you?* You don't have to learn to be fluent, although it would no doubt help; just make the effort. Effort and a friendly way are universally understood.

Frank Acuff, in his book, *How to Negotiate Anything with Anyone Anywhere Around the World,* identified seven traits that characterize American negotiators and analyzed the traits' impact on international negotiations. Many of these traits serve you well when negotiating with other Americans but may be a hindrance when you are overseas.

1. *Americans are seen as direct and open communicators.* To many people, this trait translates as being pushy and blunt. This can easily offend. Such behavior is not common in many cultures in Latin America and Asia. By being blunt, you risk missing the little things that the other side is communicating. For example, only rarely do Mexicans and Japanese answer yes or no. When the Japanese say yes they mean only that they have heard you. When they say, "That will

be difficult," they mean no. You have to judge the response in the context of what is being said, not what is actually said.

Like many Americans, many Europeans don't let emotions or relationships run the negotiations. Germans especially can be as deal-oriented as Americans. The English are also unemotional but are willing to take their time.

Many Europeans are a bit more formal than Americans in business relationships. The English tend not to appreciate personal questions, for example; Germans put great emphasis on titles, preferring to be called Herr Professor Shultz, rather than Helmut.

When in doubt, *ask*. "What would you like me to call you?" isn't a bad opening question. Better to err on the side of formality.

My advice? Relax, fight the temptation to want to "speed it up," listen more, watch more.

2. *Americans are impatient and seem rushed.* This kind of behavior can lead to unnecessary concessions by the Americans to the other side, who may be *very* patient.

Advice? *Slow down* when negotiating internationally. Don't let the other side know you are under time pressure.

3. *Americans normally negotiate alone rather than in teams.* People from other cultures may think that a lone American doesn't take the negotiations seriously and isn't very well prepared. Americans are often seen as "lone cowboys" who want to do it all and in a hurry.

My advice? Work within a team when negotiating. Break up the workload. You're at a disadvantage if you let one person try to handle the entire negotiations, because the other side will be working as a team.

4. *Americans tend to emphasize the short term, the immediate deal, instead of the long-term relationship.* This behavior probably comes from Americans' "quarterly report" mindset, whereas your foreign counterpart probably is compensated for results achieved over a period of years, not months.

Asians tend to value relationships. They trust the person with whom they are negotiating, rather than a contract, and see the agreement as the starting point, not the final solution. In some Asian countries, a signed contract can be invalidated if circumstances change.

To succeed in international negotiations, look for the long-term payoff and prove your commitment to the other side by your language and actions.

5. *Americans have limited experience with other cultures.* The perception here is that Americans are culturally myopic and arrogant. Americans are seen as people who refuse to learn about other cultures and languages.

This may be the most important problem facing Americans in international negotiations.

Again, my advice is to make an honest effort to learn about the other side's culture and language. Think of terms of making friends and building a relationship that will last over years, not just making the deal in front of you. Make the effort to understand the other side's language; fluency is nice, but an effort is crucial.

6. *Americans emphasize content over relationships.* The typical American, after exchanging pleasantries, wants to get down to business. Americans are also logical, factual, and legalistic. This attitude can easily turn off people from other cultures who place more value on building relationships. If an American doesn't take the time to build a relationship, the others may think that he has something to hide and is not trustworthy.

Again, *slow down and listen!*

7. *American negotiators are seen as excessively legalistic.* Americans tend to prefer lengthy, written contracts. This leads to a perception by others that Americans don't trust themselves or others and have to protect themselves with lengthy, wordy contracts. Negotiators from other countries, especially in the Middle East and Latin America, see this as an affront to friendship and trust.

Contracts in the Middle East are seen as only the first step in negotiations.

Most of our contracts are too lengthy and hard to read. If you need something in writing, make it short and conversational. No court ever threw out a contract because it was too easy to understand.

An American negotiator who hopes to succeed in international negotiations has to be flexible and must approach people of other cultures from their point of view. Others may expect you to act in what they see as negative American ways. Pleasantly surprise them early on in negotiations. The goodwill will serve you well throughout your relationship.

CHAPTER REVIEW

To review what have you learned, take the following open-book review quiz.

1. What are the three games every great negotiator knows how to play?

   _____

2. What are the four most important negotiating variables?

   _____

3. What mistakes of new negotiators do you sometimes make?

   _____

4. What qualities do you have that wouldn't be strengths when you are negotiating overseas?
   What specifically would you do differently when negotiating overseas?

   _____

   _____

   _____

SELECTED READINGS

Acuff, Frank. *How to Negotiate Anything with Anyone Anywhere Around the World.* New York: AMACOM Books, 1993.

Bazerman, Max H., and Margaret A. Neale. *Negotiating Rationally.* New York: Free Press, 1992.

Brooks, Earl, and George S. Odiorne. *Managing by Negotiations.* New York: Van Nostrand Reinhold, 1984.

Dawson, Roger. *Secrets of Power Negotiating.* Franklin Lakes, N.J.: Career Press, 1995.

Gottlieb, Marvin, and William J. Healy. *Making Deals.* New York: Simon & Schuster, 1990.

Maddux, Robert B. *Successful Negotiation.* Los Altos, Calif.: Crisp Publications, 1988.